Victorian Life in Photographs

Victorian Life in Photographs

Introduction by

WILLIAM SANSOM

Photographic Research by HAROLD CHAPMAN
Research Consultant JOHN HILLELSON

with 181 illustrations

THAMES AND HUDSON

Picture selection and layout by Ian Mackenzie-Kerr

© THAMES AND HUDSON 1974, LONDON
Reprinted 1980

Filmset by Tradespools Ltd., Frome, Somerset
Printed and bound in Spain by Heraclio Fournier, S.A., Vitoria.

ontents

Introduction

The Fabric of Life

ONCE UPON A TIME – and, looking back, that time seems singularly sunny.

A time of domestic peace, when life could be lived at a leisurely pace, when the world's map grew pinker and pinker as the Empire grew, when the British felt themselves to be the salt of the earth, when there was belief in Progress and families lived together and liked it. . . .

Idyllic pictures come to mind . . . in a countryside still graceful with the horse, and which truly smelled of the country, of flowering currants and the white hawthorn, of new-mown hay and violets, the mind's eye goes lily-ing in the summer shade or wooding for apple and juniper branches to scent the winter hearth . . . and the Town was brilliant with fashionable equestrian parades in the Park, with women in *mousseline* and tarlatan carrying parasols, with gaily uniformed soldiers and strolling silk-hatted gentlemen; great balls vied with immense dinner parties, with a tiara'd opera-house or the rosy plush of a spirited music hall . . . all opulent or cosy in the gaslight's kindly glow, all dreams but true enough, in part and for some.

Such visions of a Golden Age always exclude pain and distress. As the Victorian era grows more distant, so does the middle-class accidie of cold mutton for supper at the end of a long and gloomy Sunday, or the lifelong penury of the millionfold poor. Dreams see the glitter of a ballgown, seldom the red eyes bent sewing it in the sweatshop.

Atmospheres of the antique shop further obfuscate the truth. Like a badly turned piece of mahogany, the doubtful word 'Victoriana' screeches across the windowpane of our sensibilities. It is both deceptive and imprecise. It tries to embrace a vast conglomeration of objects produced over a period of more than sixty years, herding together very various fashions and styles, of which perhaps the only common factor is their production either by hand or by careful craftsmanship unknown today. However hideous the design, somehow all have come to earn the epithet 'pretty'. The whole period comes loosely to assume rose-coloured glasses.

Fifty years ago this was not so. The generations were still near enough to be glad to have escaped the gloom and the harshness, the discomfort and pious manners of a society which had largely to work excessively long hours for security and the earnest hope, so slow to be realized, of 'betterment'. Today, appealing pictures abound in the memory, like that of the scarlet-coated guardsman sauntering in the park with his pretty nurse-maid – we forget entirely that this was a once-a-week phenomenon, that the soldier lived under savage discipline in a most insanitary barracks, and that the nurse-maid was tied to her mistress's household, with little time off, for often as little as £10 a year. Yet on a more affirmative note the period was altogether one when people did enjoy simple pleasures, such as that walk in the park or an upper-class drive out in the carriage, and when families lived closely and humanly together, making up their own fun and games, playing and singing ballads at the silk-fronted piano, collecting all manner of treasures from pressed flowers to crystals and from crests to shells, reading aloud to each other, sketching and water-colouring, fancy-stitching and confecting Berlin woolwork – all that patient and creative family endeavour round the plush-draped parlour table in the glow of its glass-funnelled paraffin lamp, the cynosure which Thackeray celebrated as the safe and weather-defying 'mahogany tree'. There was thus human contact and human conversation, warm factors our present press-button age often sighs for and is startled to find revived in times of emergency. They were days, too, when infrequent evenings out at a dance or a music hall, or the very occasional holiday, were looked forward to with real fervour, trebling with anticipation the passing pleasure.

And all was set against a firm and only very slowly changing social structure, a solid fabric of life which could be labelled monotonous or peaceful according to your fortune, but which at least allowed you to see yourself clearly, sense the passage of time, appreciate the better certainties of life and improvise with all the self-help in you.

The teaching of history is chequered with periods named after formerly powerful monarchs. Such labels were once convenient, but latterly are not very helpful. In recent centuries life has been more changed by events than by the deaths and entrances of kings and queens. With Victoria, whose reign lasted sixty-four years, the period is far too long to subsist under one label, so that it comes to be divided into the rather amorphous sections 'early', 'mid' and 'late'. From a practical point of view, the true 'early' dates from the accession in 1837 to a big event in 1846, the repeal of the corn tariffs, which lowered the price of bread and began a long period of free trade. The beacon of the Prince Consort's Great Exhibition in 1851 illuminates the first years of the highly prosperous mid-Victorian period. This lasted until the mid-'seventies, when cheap mechanically reaped American corn arrived in great bulk to break England's agriculture and force large-scale emigration, and when both German and American industrialization had grown strong enough to challenge Britain's immense dominance of international trade.

However, two main common factors did distinguish the whole Victorian era. One was peace; though the regular army was involved in many campaigns abroad, from Ashanti to Burma, from the Maoris to the Matabeles, there was no major European war. The second factor was the coming of the railways, which revolutionized domestic travel and the carriage of freight. They naturally accelerated foreign trade, whose basic industries were coal, iron, steel and the consequent engineering works, all of which boomed fast and furiously during those expansive years. Not fast, though furiously debated, went many heartfelt and arduous efforts of humanitarians to alleviate the truly appalling conditions of labour in the mines and the factories. But over the slow years reforms and humane restrictions were indeed effected, together with other important matters like electoral reform; and again the railways helped in this, allowing people to see more easily what went on in different parts of the country hitherto remote in strenuous coaching days.

The girl-Queen ascended the throne of a near-Georgian nation lit largely by candle and oil, with open sewers in the streets, with unpoliced highways, with no such thing as, for instance, anaesthetics (1847). Not even an envelope – letters were sealed in wafer-thin paper, and paid for heavily by the recipient before the Penny Post of 1840. No pens but the quill, sharpened with a pen knife.

But after sixty-four years the old Queen died to a brightly gaslit world rapidly changing to electric light, to the rattle of the first motor-cars and the ringing of quite a few telephone bells. Among earlier domestic inventions, like the sewing machine and those early typewriters with their black and white piano keys, came the photographic camera. It was first deplored as a death-blow to painting. In fact it destroyed painting less than borrowed from it. Scenes were arranged like academic compositions; posing indeed matched a slow-working atmosphere when a ninety-second exposure might be necessary, and when the photographer had to carry around with him a cumbersome tent for immediate use as a dark-room. For the purposes of this book, one must largely overlook the earliest and most difficult daguerreotype period, and point to 1851 and the invention of the wet collodion plate as the beginning of easier practical photography; thence much later to the 'eighties for the general use of instantaneous roll-film.

Sunlight and shadow – these two familiar opposites were needed to make up most of the photographic record, and at the same time stand as emblems of two different faces of Victorian life, great affluence and great poverty. An anonymous jingle ran:

A boat afloat, a cloudless sky,
A nook that's green and shady,
A cooling drink, a pigeon pie,
A lobster, and a lady!

While Thomas Hood's earlier words were still equally true:

With fingers weary and worn,
With eyelids heavy and red,
A woman sat in unwomanly rags
Plying her needle and thread –

Stitch! stitch! stitch!
In poverty, hunger and dirt.

The whole Victorian picture proliferated with such opposites and schisms. Town life and country life were for long entirely separate and dissimilar. Life in the country was ruled by the squire, who owned not only the property but also the law through his position as magistrate; towns became increasingly overcrowded as farm-workers immigrated in search of better industrial wages, though civic administration was in more democratic municipal hands. A further schism, lurking like a pea-souper outside the windows of the cherished home, was religious – chapel versus church, the dissident nonconformist working class in conflict with the established church; a conflict extended by the tractarian and then Roman leanings of Newman's Oxford Movement, and much discomfited by Darwin's explosive theory of evolution. But by far the greatest schism was still represented by Disraeli's dictum that Britain was not one but two nations, Rich and Poor. It was an over-simplification, for it excluded the skilled worker and the growing middle classes, but it was still largely true. The difference may be reiterated by two word pictures – the first, a description from Disraeli's *Lothair* (1870) of the arrival of an aristocrat at his estate, where he was met at the station by 'five hundred horsemen all well mounted' who accompanied his carriage to his gates. Arrived then on the mansion's steps, he is greeted by the whole household of the Towers arranged in groups: '. . . The house steward, the chief butler, the head gardener, the chief of the kitchen, the head keeper, the head forester, and grooms of the stud and of the chambers, formed one group behind the housekeeper, a grave and distinguished-looking female, who curtseyed like the old court; half a dozen powdered gentlemen, glowing in crimson liveries, indicated the presence of my Lord's footmen, while the rest of the household, considerable in numbers, were arranged in groups according to their sex, and at a respectful distance.'

This was fiction, but based securely on fact. One of the lesser servants, for instance, would have been the steel-boy, whose sole job was to burnish the steel bits and stirrups in the stables; and there was probably the clock-man, whose only business it was to journey round the innumerable rooms of the mansion winding and superintending clocks.

In contrast to such lordly extravagance, we may observe the bottom end of the scale, the common lodging house used by lowest-paid workers like street vendors. At least they managed to conserve their liberty and avoid the discipline of a much-feared workhouse; but these common lodgers would have to share a room with some twenty others, including women and children, and pay an extra penny a night for a part share of a bed or straw palliasse, otherwise sleep on the floor; the only sanitary convenience was a slop-pail in the middle of the room, and the whole place was a breeding ground for bugs, lice and fleas, compelling a newly conceived Board of Health at least to order the walls to be whitewashed.

Between these two extremes of powdered flunkeys and 'whitewashed' walls, there came into being the immense new dimension of the Victorian middle class. We may observe from Cruikshank's engraving of *The British Bee Hive* how highly services to home comfort were esteemed; tradesmen and others, from cheesemonger to coalheaver, take up three whole rows of the hive, compared with only two cells given over to 'work for men and boys', in fact the basic heavy industries which really made the hive hum. The middle classes, engineers and shopkeepers and clerical workers, are seen to give their useful services to the bee hive – but the most populous kind of all servants is left out, the domestic. It is startling to note that the number of domestic servants (1,039,000 in 1851) is only exceeded by that of agricultural labourers, and totalled twice that of all mill operatives. A large proportion of these domestics served the middle classes who could afford to keep a maid. The pay was little; but service was not then an indignity; a girl thought herself lucky to obtain a secure post, with food and board, and protection against the rigours of the hard world outside.

Altogether the Victorians cannot be blamed for accepting near-slave conditions in labour and service; there had always been a traditional distinction between the unfortunate and the fortunate, between poor and prosperous. It was a fact of life. When the provident sat by a good coal fire, blazing so hot as to need a painted glass firescreen, they hardly dwelled on thoughts of the pregnant woman whose belt and chain had dragged those same coals through a cramping narrow tunnel deep in the dark earth. Nor did they pause to consider the heavy iron scuttles of coals which the maid had to carry up many stairs each day. These were simply hard but necessary conditions. They could only be slowly changed, if ever. Not too much blame, then: but praise indeed for the working humanitarians like Lord Ashley (later Shaftesbury) who did realize the harshness of the worst distress, who refused to tolerate it, and worked throughout their lives to relieve suffering. Among notable instances of their success there occurred in the 'forties Acts excluding women, and children under ten, from underground work in the mines (1842), and in 1847 limiting the work in textile factories to ten hours per day. Rigorous enough still by our lights; but then a positive step forward, particularly because such laws stimulated regular government inspection of suspect conditions.

The early years of Victoria's reign, which one might visually assess as precrinoline days, were scarcely as pretty as the elegant house-furnishings of the period. The high price of protected corn made the time known as the Hungry Forties. Bread was the staple diet of the millions, who were now driven to eat for a time yellow maize bread, known as 'Peel's Brimstone'. In Ireland 1845 saw the potato crop failure and consequent famine, where thousands died of starvation. Open rebellion was feared at home and stimulated by the Chartist riots. In 1848 these were to culminate in the calling of a mass meeting on Kennington Common of an expected half-million ready to march north of the Thames. The Court found it advisable to retire to Osborne House on the tighter little Isle of Wight; clerks in government offices were issued with muskets, and artillery lined the north bank from Waterloo Bridge to Millwall. Unaccountably, only a twentieth of the expected supporters turned up at Kennington, and the march was abandoned. The material danger was past, and was not to occur again. The six points of the original Charter aimed for a more democratic Parliament, ranging from complete male suffrage to the payment of elected members. All points, with the exception of annually elected parliaments, have over the years been accepted. The year 1848 was one of violent revolution throughout much of Europe, including a usually stable Germany. Historians still debate the failure of Britain's oppressed to erupt, dividing their theories between a less excitable temperament and unimaginative, impractical leadership.

Meanwhile the Court at Windsor, though splendid and rich, was already setting its example of family devotion, sobriety and morality which was to be reflected throughout Victoria's reign in the generally earnest strictures of middle-class family life. Soon the walls of thousands of parlours would bear, illuminated in an Oxford frame, the exhortation: 'God Bless Our Home'. 'Albert der King', as he was first unpopularly known, proved to be a recessive man of serious mind, who diplomatically kept himself in the political background, while working strenuously on the safer educational and scientific projects which culminated in his conception and presidency of the Great Exhibition of 1851. An example of Victoria's own social attitude is found in her disapproval of traditional heavy male drinking after dinner, requesting the presence of the gentlemen only a quarter of an hour after the ladies had left the table. Drinking habits in polite society certainly quietened during Victorian years, when reinforced ports and madeiras gradually gave way to claret and hock. Early Victorians did not take tea, but wine and cake in the afternoon. Hot gin was a lady's extra stimulant, and many a flask of brandy knew the darkness of the reticule. Drink was always relatively cheap, with a quart of the dark beer at 3d, and we find, though much later in the century, the small suburban clerkly figure of Mr. Pooter buying from the grocer cheap champagne at 3/6d a bottle. For the proletariat, drink offered an evil oblivion whenever conditions of living became unbearable. It was not uncommon to see children haplessly drunk. Babies were quietened with gin.

In early-Victorian days, the pleasures of Society were taken largely at home with huge dinners of many assorted courses, or with the candlelit or gaslit glitter of private balls. Almack's Assembly Rooms provided a unique alternative, where balls were given every Wednesday under the supervision of six Lady Patronesses, elegant affairs of cotillion and quadrille so exclusive that even the Duke of Wellington could be denied entry for being late. Otherwise, fashionable nightlife centred on the Vauxhall and later the Cremorne Gardens, where among gorgeously contrived pavilions lit with lanterns pleasure-seekers could stroll, listen to music, watch the fireworks or, a favourite event, the ascent of balloons. But Vauxhall and Cremorne were not exclusive, and, as with other 'tea' or pleasure gardens scattered further afield, were finally closed because of unruly behaviour, Cremorne lasting until 1877. It seems to have been an English particular not to be able to sustain with decorum the dual temptations of night and the open air.

We still derive the phrase 'legitimate theatre' from those early days, when straight drama (including Shakespeare) was only legitimately permitted at three theatres in London, Drury Lane, Covent Garden and, in summer only, the Haymarket. Elsewhere, theatres had by law to leaven what drama there was with music and song, developing a lighter type of performance known as a burletta. The law was not rescinded until 1843. The play was in any case limited by gas and candle lighting, which could not be lowered in the auditorium, and by the noise of the fashionable parade strolling the orchestra stalls. Actors were forced to overact and make their situations visually plain by cast-iron gesture, much as in early silent films. But at another form of theatre, Astley's circus, Charles Dickens in *The Old Curiosity Shop* (1840) notes: 'What a glow was that, which burst upon them all, when that long, clear, brilliant row of lights came slowly up.' He notes the carrying of apples and oranges kitted up in handkerchiefs, of the wonder of the paint, gilding and looking-glass and 'the vague smell of horses suggestive of coming wonders'. The performance seems to have been a mixture of circus and play, with '. . . the pony who reared up on his hind legs when he saw the murderer, and wouldn't hear of walking on all-fours again until he was taken in custody . . . the lady who jumped over the nine-and-twenty ribbons and came down safe on the horse's back. . . .' After the play Kit's party walk into an oyster shop nearby and occupy 'a private box, fitted up with red curtains, white table-cloth, and cruet-stand complete' for three dozen of largest-size oysters and a pot of beer. Oysters were then commonly four a penny. Mr. Pickwick took a barrel of them down for Christmas at Dingley Dell.

But it is time to pass from early Pickwickian days – Pickwick acceded to the printed page in the same year of the Queen's accession to the throne – when men still wore bright-coloured coats and pantaloons, and pass to the mid-Victorian period which more largely concerns the earlier photographs in this collection. For two decades, the 'fifties and 'sixties, we enter a very different world of tall tophats, staid frock-coats and enormous crinolines, as affluence and inventive progress greased the wheels of the Victorian Age to speed free of a Georgian hangover; wheels which alongside the ubiquitous horse traffic included 5,000 miles of railway by 1848, with many more thousands authorized, reaching a total of about 22,000 miles at the century's end.

Railways and coal: house chimneys and the chimneys of locomotives and steamers seem symbolically to be echoed by a factor which instantly now strikes the eye – those extraordinarily tall and unwieldy tophats of the men of this middle period. Such preponderant funnels increased a man's height and gave him a most officious and forbidding aspect. He was crowned in black with the emblem of prosperity: and though in fact the hat's great size reduced the wearer's actual features, you might have thought it belched an invisible smoke of effort and industry as he bore down on you. It connoted, too, a fetish of respectability – and some might suggest of priapic fertility – and was worn on every possible occasion. Onto the cricket field it went, above the white shirt of the player; a shopkeeper might wear one behind his counter; and it was always carried into the drawing-room on a visit, as if inseparable from its loving owner. It was worn indoors in men's clubs. In the streets, there was a constant doffing and donning, doffed *clear* of the head if addressed to a lady. And in those rougher days, in the event of attack from a bully's cudgel, or in the accidental stress of a not infrequent overturning of gig or carriage, the hat became a crash-helmet.

At the same time the ladies began to sport a complementary visual extravagance, the crinoline skirt which sometimes measured as much as twelve feet round the bottom hem. It developed from previous padded and many-petticoated skirts; the pads were made of horsehair, or *crin*, the obvious source of the word 'crinoline', though in fact the new hooped steel cage obviated the neces-

14

sity of pads. Many petticoats were still worn to set the outer dress properly, but now the legs were free in laced pantaloons reaching to the ankle, and in profile this extraordinary skirt, whose popularity lasted about twenty years, gave the effect of a triangle whose base might measure the same as the wearer's height, and whose gliding footless carriage depended at best on the lady's personal deportment. At times, though, it would billow about like a rogue balloon, allowing the passing gentleman an enticingly erotic view of the ankle garments and the new boots then coming to be worn. But on the whole the crinoline's rounded implacability made a redoubtable fortress of its unattainable wearer, allowing an arm's length touch of the hand though not easily an embrace, and indeed taking up so much space that it was impossible to sit beside a lady on a sofa; many sofas were in any case designed for people sitting apart, with a backless division between, or as the S-shaped back-to-back pieces called 'unsociables'. The crinoline was also useful for cheating at croquet, and as a curiosity inevitably attracted the joke-monger – even lovers were laughingly concealed beneath such conveniently capacious tents.

Bonnets, pill-boxes, pork-pie and other relatively brimless hats kept the apex of such a triangular woman small. The corsage was worn flat, discreetly cancelling the shape of the bosom. Parasols and in winter muffs were carried, coral and jet jewellery was popular, and the whole silken ensemble now conjures up a sweetly romantic propriety. Yet at the same time this was one of the most horrific eras of prostitution ever known. Many thousands of bonneted and crinolined whores pressed nightly into the advantageous London centre of the Haymarket and Regent Street. The so-called 'sporting' gentleman, in his dark frock-coat and white duck or checked trousers, his fancy waistcoat and long Dundreary whiskers, left the puritan rigours of desk or domestic hearth to entertain himself in an absolutely different nightworld of oyster saloons and smoking divans, the Cyder cellars and such dance and supper places as the Argyll Rooms or Kate Hamilton's infamous night-house in Panton Street. 'Are you feeling good-natured, sir?' was the nicely polite query from the solicitous passing bonnet.

The crinolined wife, whose place was unquestionably the home and the child-bearing bed, took to daytime shopping streets very different from today's. In many urban districts one may still see rows of Victorian houses with a small iron device let into the front doorpost, in fact a foot-scraper. This was for mud. Most of the streets were neither stone-setted nor macadamized. The crinoline's hem had to traverse roads churned and puddled with soot-dark mud and a ceaseless weight of horse-droppings. Neither the hordes of scavenging sparrows nor the street 'orderlies' employed by the Vestries (today's Borough Councils) could keep such streets properly clean and passable. So at certain corners, sometimes provided with stone-laid crossings, there stood a crossing-sweeper, often a boy or otherwise one of the poorest of the poor, who cleared a way with his broom for a halfpenny or very occasionally a shining silver sixpence from regular customers. 'I wear out three brooms in a week,' said a sweeper interviewed by that master of mid-Victorian mass observation, Henry Mayhew, 'but in summer one will last a fortnight. I give threepence ha'penny for them.' And the daily takings would be as little as a shilling, or at the best half-a-crown. Bad weather and winter were welcomed by the sweeper; they made for more work despite the hardship of standing all day soaked and shivering.

Mud naturally mounted the pavements, so that a shopping expedition needed a lot of cleaning and brushing afterwards at home. The shops themselves were small-windowed, and many of their wares, from baskets and pails to sides of meat and poultry, were hung in profusion outside. Nothing was ready-wrapped at the grocer's: the butter stood in high mounds which had to be cut and moulded by two wooden patters which clacked a deft music long forgotten now; bacon was sliced by hand, coarse white sugar came in cones which had to be scissored and sold in bulk to be broken into lumps later at home; tea, an expensive item, came from chests, and was destined for locked caddies in the mistress's charge; lentils, flour, beans, rice were all scooped from sacks, barrels or jars, and then carefully weighed on brass hand-scales before being wrapped not in bags but in cones of dark brown paper, twisted close at the top. Coffee was ground personally from the bean. But many foods were tasted and examined by the shopping wife, and most necessarily, too. Adulteration was widespread. The Sanitary Commission of 1855 found starch and flour in cocoa, red lead and ochre in cayenne pepper, as much as fifty per cent added water in milk, insects and fungi in sugar, preserved fruits contaminated with copper and confectionery with chlorate of lead. Bread was laced with alum to hold more water and weigh more.

Yet the Victorian shop at least smelled of its wares in a lively way, from the mixed odours of coffee and soap and spices at the grocer's to the muffling smell of 'stuffs' at the draper's or milliner's; and shopping proved at least to be one of the small reliefs for a woman so largely tied to her home. Contact with the shopkeeper and other shoppers could be pleasantly personal, gossip and idle chatter welcomed as a blessing. To and fro the home was largely on foot – the Victorians were in any case great walkers, country children plodded many miles to school, and clerks often economized by striding all the way from suburb to city desk on foot. But there were times when the housewife took one of the small horse-drawn omnibuses, in which her equipage of crinoline and parcels proved a formidable embarrassment. Trollope notes with some venom: 'The woman, as she enters, drags after her a misshapen, dirty mass of battered wirework, which she calls her crinoline . . . of this she takes much heed, not managing it so that it may be conveyed up the carriage with some decency, but striking it against men's legs, and heaving it with violence over people's knees. The touch of a real woman's dress is in itself delicate; but these blows from a harpy's fin are loathsome.'

Many classes of shop have in the main long disappeared, like the saddler's so vital to a horse-trotting age, and the gutta-percha shops selling all kinds of rubber commodities from shoe soles to imitation wood, and the old kind of oil-shop with its two red fascia jars labelled 'Linseed and Colza Oils'. There was the plumassier's selling swansdown and osprey feathers and brightly coloured trimmings; and salivating smells rose from the pie-man's, whose large trade was not in pork but in mutton pies. For the improvident, the three brass balls of the pawnbroker's were much more common than nowadays; together with the striped pole of the barber's, and the huge red, yellow and purple flasks of coloured liquids illuminating a druggist's window. But opposite this line of shops with their gold-lettered names and the convex white enamel messages on their windows, stood another line of vendors in the gutter: the vast army of itinerant street-sellers, offering on trays or barrows cutlery, prints, magazines, tape, thread, buttons, fruit, medicinal rhubarb and spice, coconuts, and much, much else. Behind these marched the sandwich-board men, advertising theatres or circuses or patent medicines, and thought by one Chinese observer to be undergoing an official punishment encased thus in such brutal boards strapped to their shoulders. And on the pavements between the glass-windowed shops and the gutter-trade came other itinerant traders – the water-cress girl, the lavender and herb girl, the glazier with his astounding burden of glass sheets, and such as the rabbit-seller with his poles strung with rabbits or the oyster-seller with a barrel on his head; and always that beloved benefactor of the tea-time hour, the muffin man ringing his bell and bearing on his head a cloth-covered tray piled with fresh-baked muffins and crumpets.

So, with occasional pockets of acrobats, stilt-dancers, dancing bears, ballad-singers selling songsheets by the yard and even the lame old soldier doing his rifle exercises, it was a turbulent main street for the tophatted gentlemen and their bell-skirted ladies booting it along mud-sludged pavements. Not all the above all at once, of course, but enough of them to enliven the passing scene in a way we do not know today. And beyond this din and clatter, above the hurrying street urchin and the pertinacious pickpocket, rose a high and passing edifice on the road itself, the dense and extraordinary tall horse-traffic of the time. You could seldom see the other side of the street for the high-perched drivers of victorias, hansoms, broughams, landaus, gigs, omnibuses, barge-shaped coal-carts, brewers' drays, carts of all kinds from manure carts to tradesmen's carts and advertising vans, and even sometimes the great six-horsed country wain.

Horses were often bigger and heavier than we know, and the brewer's dray, with its muscular driver in his smock and red stocking-cap, was the heavy-weight of a road which seldom echoed to the isolated bright clip-clop of merry hooves on cobbles but more to a grinding and heaving of huge iron-shod wheels and the gee-up cries and whip-cracking of drivers, who even fought each other with their whips in a jam or when the wheels, as often they did, became inter-locked. So great was the tireless and tyreless din that straw was frequently laid across the street opposite the houses of the very ill. Traffic jams could be much worse than today, considering the space a whole horse and carriage took up compared with a motor-car. Horses were beasts that slipped and fell, often causing lengthy hold-ups. On the emptier streets, they sometimes panicked and became runaways; the hero flinging himself at the wild muzzle just in time was a novelettist's cliché. Horses, too, carried their fodder bags and watering pails, littering the streets further with hay as they groaned by; and for the driver the end of a long day did not simply mean reaching garage doors but the further job of unharnessing, wiping down, feeding and blanketing the beast for the night.

The black-lacquered hansom cab with its brass fittings was known as 'the gondola of London'. Light-horsed, its two wheels nipped nicely in and out the denser traffic. In bad weather an oilcloth or leather shield was drawn right across its open seat for two, excluding all view, even of the horse's engaging rump and the reins travelling up through metal loops to the heavy-coated driver perched up behind. Slower and heavier was the four-seater four-wheeler or 'growler' descended from the earlier hackney coach. There were also cabs for a single passenger, called after their shape 'coffin-cabs', with the driver seated at the side. Other than all these black-painted hackney-cabs, which only very slowly took to a fare-recording taximeter, the ordinary form of public transport was the brightly coloured omnibus seating twelve inside and four-teen on the 'knifeboard' or back-to-back seats on the top. These top seats were reached in earlier days by almost vertical iron ladders clamped so that no lady and only the more agile male could manage the climb. Later the seats were rearranged to face forwards in rows, and a rudimentary stairway was set curling to the top.

In 1861 the American Mr. Train gave London its first tram. It ran only a short distance along the Bayswater road, but was soon multiplied by a number of privately run companies which saw the value of a greater passenger capacity and an easier haulage strain for the coupled horses. No steam trams until the 'eighties: but a year as early as 1863 saw the opening of the Metropolitan Underground Railway, which first ran in open trucks through the smoke-filled tunnels, bearing with it, among other tophatted dignitaries, Mr. Gladstone. Yet as late as 1887, the diarist R. D. Blumenfeld was to record of an underground coach on the same line: 'The compartment in which I sat was filled with passengers who were smoking pipes, as is the British habit, and as the smoke and sulphur from the engine fill the tunnel, all the windows have to be closed. The atmosphere was a mixture of sulphur, coal dust and foul fumes from the oil lamp above; so that by the time we reached Moorgate Street I was near dead of asphyxiation and heat. I should think these Underground railways must soon be discontinued, for they are a menace to health.' Plainly no picnic.

Home life in the 'fifties and 'sixties was for the middle classes largely geared to the number of servants one could afford. For the upper-income professional man, or one of the many thousands whose profession was leisure, a very large retinue became necessary, both for the parade of wealth and to be able to run one of the numerous and huge four- or five-storey mansions lining the streets of big cities. Often, for appearance's sake, a footman's livery cost far more than his master's outfit. All servants lived in strict hierarchical pecking order under the control of the butler and cook or housekeeper; they mostly slept at the top of the house, and worked from ill-lit basements. But the more of them the mildly merrier for their daily lives; despite incessant hard work and low wages, they would make up a below-stairs human family; there was daily contact with tradesmen, who might be offered a mug of 'small beer', and the policeman-cook relationship was not the joke it has since become but a properly cordial acquaintance between the basement-bound and the regular passer-by. A life of unrelieved loneliness and drudgery was more likely in the household with only one or two servants; a lot then depended on the mistress's personality, which plainly could be tyrannous. The amount of work was vast. Cooking was by coal-fired range, and the whole house was heated by coal which had to be carried by hand. The kitchen table of white deal and the wooden draining board at the sink had to be scoured, and the copper pans burnished daily. There would be a bricked-in copper for boiling the weekly wash, a mangle for drying plus a long wooden rack lowered by pulleys from the ceiling. No steel was stainless; all knives had to be cleaned with knife powder and polished, often in a round drum-like machine containing brushes and revolved by a handle. Together with all the other equipments to keep clean, from jelly moulds to cake tins, there was a whole industry of jam-making, fruit-preserving, pickling, wine-making, cake and sometimes bread baking, and even the making of shoe and furniture polishes ordered for economy's sake. So the kitchen became also a kind of laboratory; and indeed the chemistry of cleaning, with all its variants of beeswax for this or soft soap for that, was better understood than today with its destructively sharp detergents.

Thus the kitchen alone – upstairs lay another whole world of brushing and polishing of furniture and grates, sweeping and dusting and water-carrying; no baths – hip baths were set in front of a bedroom fire, to which many cans of hot water had to be carried. Dusting alone was a pernicious task in homes crammed with davenports, whatnots, work-baskets and a profusion of pictures, vases and multitudinous decorative objects difficult nowadays to comprehend. Everything, in those extremely sooty and foggy days, when in winter the gaslight was often turned up at midday, had to be lifted, cleaned and exactly replaced. And there were the front and back doorbells to be answered, those iron bell-pulls whose long wires actuated a carillon of little bells set high on the wall near the kitchen; and also an ear kept open for such street cries as 'Milk-oh!' from the milkman who might still have no cart but carry his pails on a wooden yoke. Day-to-day life was altogether a momentous task allowing little leisure at all; and of course the daughters of the house would be engaged too on the less menial jobs.

As can still be seen today in the vast residue of Victorian terrace building, rooms were bigger, and more ponderous were safety devices like the miles of heavy iron railings. Fearfully the silver was locked away nightly in big mahogany cases and carried to upstairs cupboards. Many lower windows were shuttered inside; and this indicates one remarkable difference between the use of Victorian houses in their heyday and today – the Victorians kept themselves much warmer. The shutters served as a kind of double-glazing, and altogether each window was heavily rigged with oil-cloth blinds, or Venetian jalousies, and very thick plush curtains, all of which kept the heat in. Even interior doors were often furnished with heavy draught-curtains on a brass rod. Coal was cheap and burned fiercely, while much clothing was worn by both sexes at home, women and men taking easily to shawls and knee rugs, mittens, mufflers, bedsocks, often indeed wearing headgear, such as a mob-cap or a smoking-cap, indoors. Woollen night-caps were worn in beds heated by stone hot water bottles. Beds were cosy, if frequently flea-catching, with warmly enveloping feather mattresses. So today such houses, with their sash window-frames shrunk over the years, give little feeling of the snugness of their earlier years.

Chocolate or dark maroon paint was widely used for whole house façades, or for window-frames in brick houses. Though gloomy, it provided some protection against the prevailing sootiness and fog. Such colours also entered the houses, along with yellow-brown paint like grained oak, as a means of minimizing the knock-marks of brooms and brushes. Today's repainting in white gives a totally inaccurate impression of Victorian rooms, where common sense and thrift prevailed over brightness. Nor was the outside street scene bright with coloured pictorial posters; hoardings were covered with a dully dizzying mass of lettering, often surmounted by permanent announcements in more lettering painted on commercial walls, some of which, much faded, can still be seen today.

Even the best-ordered home could not cope properly with indifferent sanitary conditions. The water closet was largely in use, but the pipes themselves tended to leak, and easily blocked drains threw up noisome gases causing many a sore throat; curiously, such drains were even liked and respected for foretelling bad weather when they stank more than usual. The poorer slums, in rookeries where a case is recorded in central London of 1,000 people inhabiting 26 three-storey houses, were served only with overflowing cesspits and open drains. When Windsor Castle, not exactly a rookery, was being renovated in the 'forties, no less than fifty-three over-filled cesspools were found underneath. London's overtaxed drainage went straight into the Thames, which inevitably smelled like the sewer it was, so much so that in the hot summer of 1858 the riverside blinds of the Houses of Parliament had to be soaked with chloride of lime. The fear of cholera was constant. There had already been severe outbreaks. Drinking water was analysed under the microscope to show an enormous population of what were then called 'insects' – specimens of which were even on show at popular exhibition arcades such as the Pantheon. This water was drawn from the Thames itself. Filtered water was specially on sale – as at the Crystal Palace, where only non-alcoholic drinks were permitted. In 1853 there had occurred, for only one instance, a further cholera epidemic in London, when eleven and a half thousand died; but because of deep-laid dislikes of interference with private property and state control, the whole matter of sanitation took until 1870 to be accelerated and until the century's end to be put reasonably right. Drinking water was known as 'stinking water' – and among the plush overmantles and the china ornaments, the ottomans and the lace curtains, life and health were assuredly at risk.

When progress lay in private rather than official hands, nothing delayed it. The railways offer the prime example, so speedily built that they over-estimated themselves, stimulating a 'railway mania' for shares which too frequently became worthless. The great engineer Isambard Kingdom Brunel marks an example of one man's vision, tenacity and expansive enterprise. Immense bridges, tunnels, railway termini, even the first ocean-going screw steamer – edifices of iron, stone and brick rose with no delay among the forests of his scaffolding, until the laying down at Millwall of his largest achievement, the

Great Eastern steamship. Its tonnage was so huge for the time that finally it was only launched after three failures and even then, in 1858, was nearly abandoned; finally this monstrous vessel laid the first transatlantic cable. Yet England, a maritime island with still few ironclads in its navy, continued to build great sailing ships, like the *Cutty Sark*, as late as 1869. Meanwhile the cotton mills of Lancashire and the kilns of the Potteries were multiplying and improving, and mechanical energy extended in new directions – steam presses for printing in the 'fifties, and steam engines in the fields for threshing. Yet still at the turn of the century much reaping was done by scythe and sickle, and in some southern counties oxen still pulled the plough long into Edwardian days. The whole Victorian era was thus one of violent, exhaustive change peppered with pockets of tradition dying hard indeed.

A paramount instance of these opposites may be felt from the Crimean War period. First, in 1851, came the Great Exhibition. Apart from its merchandizing vision, its six million visitors and financial success, the building itself was phenomenal – a prefabricated glass and iron structure covering eighteen acres and high enough to enclose full-grown elms. Four hundred tons of glass, four thousand tons of iron. Outside, in one of the main avenues, stood a symbolical single block of coal weighting 24 tons. Apart from an often laughable xenophobia, which even advocated the supply to London of vast new public lavatories to accommodate foreigners of unreliable habit, the grand intention of the Exhibition was to further peace and understanding between the nations of the world. Yet three years later, with enthusiastic popular approval, a courageous but ill-equipped expeditionary force was dispatched to the Crimea. This army, not much changed since Napoleonic campaigns and despite severe lessons learned in the Crimea, was not finally reorganized until the Cardwell reforms of the early 'seventies, when among much else the antiquated purchase of commissions was at last abolished; though flogging, long considered a barbarism abroad, continued until 1881. However, despite such traditional lethargy, the war produced one great advance in the services and inspiration of Florence Nightingale, whose example opened up the conception of women becoming nurses at home in peacetime. This was an important ideological step forward on the long road to female emancipation; but any real progress, in spite of John Stuart Mill's *Subjection of Women* (1869) and the opening of women's university colleges, had to wait until very much later. The middle-class mind concerned itself above all else with the maintenance of Respectability. Unusual concepts of freedom bowed before the observant eye at the neighbour's window, and it was as vital to preserve every appearance of a station in life raised above the lower labouring classes as to wear a backboard strapped to the spine for a properly acceptable deportment.

Urban amusement for the lady was circumscribed and refined. There were the niceties of archery or croquet outdoors, or a visit – never without a chaperon – to the Zoological Gardens or Madame Tussaud's waxwork emporium then in Baker Street. Panoramic shows called dioramas or cycloramas both astonished and instructed – one might see exhibited on immense areas of illuminated canvas enthralling views of 'Paris by Moonlight' or 'The Lisbon Earthquake' at the Colosseum in Regent's Park. A huge globe was erected in Leicester Square, in which a relief map of the whole world could be viewed from an internal staircase. More startling were wondrous exhibitions, such as at the Egyptian Hall or the Adelaide Gallery, which mixed paintings and statuary with such varied attractions as a 'Lady Organist' and an 'Automaton Singing Bird in a cage of pure gold'.

Powerful sabbatarian strictures forced even Lord Palmerston, against his own will, to forbid Sunday concerts of innocent military band music in the parks. Similarly, a number of excursion trains were outlawed on Sundays. A fierce morality burned beneath those tall tophats, and religious controversy and conscience formed very real talking points for the ordinary man. Not until 1871 were universities opened to undergraduates who had not signed the thirty-nine articles of the established Anglican Church. Religion helped to engender an earnest and serious approach to life and work; an industrious disposition, upon which much of Britain's prosperity was founded, was continually encouraged in such exhortations as the following from Samuel Smiles's *Self-Help* (1859):

'As steady application to work is the healthiest training for every individual, so is the best discipline of a state. Honourable industry travels the same road with duty; and Providence has closely linked both with happiness. The gods, says the poet, have placed labour and toil in the way leading to the Elysian fields.'

Unctuous reading today, indeed: but such attitudes were then very real and go a long way to explain the stern expressions on so many of the faces in these photographs, and the unsmiling demeanour of the women with their sallow-seeming skins, their tired eyes and rougeless pale lips. Hindsight, though, may suggest that much of that current congratulation of an industrious life was a comforting sublimation of fear – fear of the neighbour's eye, fear of hell fire, fear of losing work at a time when clerks still addressed the boss as 'Master' and farmers tugged a respectful forelock to the squire.

The moral probity of the ladies was nurtured by Mudie's Select Lending Library, which circulated only the most improving and innocuous novels, relying much on the work of such writers as Charlotte M. Yonge and Mrs. Henry Wood. Though even Mr. Mudie had finally to capitulate to a reaction personified by Ouida with her seductively exotic heroines and glamorous Guards officers. The full-blooded work of Dickens had of course always been popular; but this too, within its spirited characterization, moralized on the plight of the poor and oppressed. Tennyson, with his sonorous love of nature and his consoling belief in the superiority of man, was the most read poet. Painting, from Landseer to the Pre-Raphaelites, stayed devoted to realism and the depiction of right sentiment and moral message. Architecture was much affected by the Anglican Church; the larger public buildings like town halls, museums and railway stations turned to decorative gothic or castellated romantic in an anti-classical reaction invoked to some extent by John Ruskin. But if, passing over eye-catchers built of William Butterfield's blue, red and yellow brick, we survey the real relic of mass domestic building, the style remains mostly italianate, and the amount of Victorian gothic much less than is commonly thought. If building generally became more portentous, the same was true of interiors, whose furniture grew heavier and less elegant, sacrificing proportion to ostentation, producing such familiar visions as the mid-Victorian dining-room with its massive mahogany table, its great sideboards and lordly epergnes, dark red wallpaper and heavily gilded paintings of Highland cattle or monstrous mounds of slaughtered game.

The Empire continued to grow far afield, explorers like Livingstone and Speke penetrated dangerously unknown territories, and after the Indian Mutiny (during which, as if to emphasize the separation of home and abroad, the great bell for Westminster's clock tower was drawn peaceably thither by sixteen cart-horses) the subcontinent settled down to decades of relative quiet under the surveillance of a new type of public schoolboy distilled from Dr. Arnold's model of Rugby. The beer-drinking, bullying earlier days of Eton were largely past: now games, rectitude and the team spirit came to the fore, and they did then produce the type of official able and ready to carry the vaunted White Man's Burden. But education for the masses had been neglected, left mostly in the hands of voluntary church schools aided by a minimal state grant. Not until the 'seventies and 'eighties was a system of universal primary education developed by law. And not the least reason for this was the Reform Bill of 1867 and its enfranchisement for the first time of working men, producing the dictum that 'we must educate our masters'. Then, in 1874, the Trades Unions were given the legal right to order strikes.

Throughout the three first decades and more of the reign, the names of Melbourne, Peel, Palmerston and Gladstone had reverberated like stentorian organ blasts throughout the changing times. Now from the 'seventies on, social changes were to accelerate. Disraeli's first powerful ministry took effect from 1874, coinciding with Britain's great agricultural decline under American competition, which reduced the corn-growing areas from eight million acres in 1875 to under six millions by the turn of the century. Frozen meat from the colonies lowered the profitability of land turned to grazing. A further crowding into the towns and a desperate upturn in the emigration figures resulted. Nevertheless, Britain as a whole continued to prosper, owning as much as a third of world shipping. And new towns were built, sanitation improved, wages were higher, housing if not good became at least more provident, and with greater safety on the common street manners became gentler. Emblematically the Queen's popularity, hitherto threatened by several assassination attempts and by the rumblings of republicanism, improved as she reduced the severity of her long period of mourning and appeared in public again; the Prince of Wales was ambivalently admired for his jovial manner and journeys abroad, booed for his involvement in a notorious divorce case, yet the object of national concern during his illness of 1872, when a man was nearly lynched for publicly decrying him. The Queen's Jubilees of 1887 and 1897 were finally celebrations of mass approval.

The crinoline had gone, the bustle arrived, and by the 'nineties those huge feathered and fruit- and bird-carrying hats came into vogue, along with leg-o'-mutton sleeves. The ordinary man, often bearded and smoking a 'paper cigar' or cigarette since the Crimean War, wore a cut-away coat; the tophat had been slimmed to more reasonable dimensions, and the new felt hat, sometimes known as the bowler, was in common use right down to the bootblack boy. A senior business man would still ride his cob all the way from the suburbs to the City. Extraordinarily, it was not until 1890 that the brighter gas mantle came into use, preceding by only a few years a gradual introduction of electric lighting. By the 'eighties the first telephone exhanges had arrived on a scene which still featured the evening lamplighter running with his ladder from gas-lamp to gas-lamp. Bicycling became popular, first with the cumbersome penny-farthing, of which a formidable military posse may be seen on Plate *168*, and then more so with the ordinary bone-shaker which, given a pneumatic tyre in the late 'eighties, let the low-paid townsman and woman out freely for a day in the country for the first time. Now women left the demure croquet lawn for the freer athleticism of lawn tennis; tennis parties, with young men in attendance, became the rage for both sporting and romantic reasons. The seaside holiday, with its horse-drawn and copiously canopied bathing machines, grew more and more possible and popular. If we look in disbelief at scenes of beaches crowded with overdressed holiday-makers carrying even solid household chairs with them, we forget that people were enjoying not only a real change of air but also particularly an invaluable rest from the year's drudgery of a six-day week and a decorously ordered Sunday.

One most important evidence of the growing loosening of conventions can be seen in the enormous new popularity of the music hall. A number had indeed been built in the 'sixties, but London alone saw nearly three hundred and fifty open by the last decade of the century. The charge could be as little as sixpence a seat for an uproarious night's entertainment. With flaring gas-jets and bawdy songs they bounced with conviviality; people felt a real affection for the performers, a hundred well-known names from The Great Vance to Marie Lloyd, and welcomed the repetition of the same old songs year after year: no nervous reaching for novelty then.

Women now went out to dine, so that in the West End of London the rough pews of chophouses grew fewer as elegant restaurants, gilded and mirrored, were opened – Frascati's, the Criterion, Romano's with its exotic Moorish decorations. Shops assumed brass-lined plate-glass windows, and the first large department stores attracted ladies who at last could venture out without a chaperon. Yet it was still a horse-drawn world, beggars begged, street music still echoed from Italian organ-grinders and Italian bagpipers, from nigger minstrels (earlier, 'Ethiopian Serenaders') and German brass bands. Street cries persisted – one of the oddest being that of the cat's-meat man pushing his barrow of horse-flesh. And still in the smaller home those two most distinctive Victorian smells coloured the air – the steamy smell of wet cloth on wash-day, and the sharp early-morning bouquet of burning paper and kindling wood as the fires were lit for another coal-consuming, fog-building winter's day.

Yet the look of the home was changing. As always, the middle classes eventually imitated the fashions of their superiors. And now, long after Swinburne had ceased to shock, Japanese fans and blue and white porcelain of the Aesthetic Movement rarefied the ordinary home. Art Nouveau, with its elongated lily and strange whiplash designs, breathed a lighter air among the older heavy furnishings. Baths, with their often erratic copper geysers, became more common. In 1898 the Prince of Wales took his first motor ride, and a year earlier the first electric cab was licensed as 'a mechanical Clarence'. In 1896 the first very short motion picture was shown, and at that time a Brownie camera was on sale for five shillings.

But just before the turn of this great nineteenth century the Boer War came to lower Britain's prestige abroad. It was the first time in Victoria's reign that the country as a whole had felt itself involved in war, and, although eventually it was won in a physical sense, many factions criticized its essence from the beginning and there was bred a most un-Victorian feeling of doubt.

To such uneasy music, the century turned. In 1901 the Queen died, and the Victorian Age, with its near doubling of the population, its formidably swift commercial expansion and its slower but earnest social reforms, was over.

The Victorian Camera:
Development and Technique

WE LIVE IN AN AGE which takes for granted its own immortality and which can produce each day with ease and facility enduring millions of images of its acts and postures, its environments, whether they be terrestrial, spatial, submarine or microscopic, its artifacts, its flora and fauna; it is easy to forget that only a very short time ago the notion that our reflections could ever be given any permanence at all was merely a dream goading several obsessed men through years of experiment in primitive home-made laboratories.

Today, a barely literate child can produce a recognizable image in fairly realistic colour of his parents caught in a fleeting gesture. He has merely to press the button; the precision-built camera, the throw-away flash bulb and the efforts of a great industrial complex do the rest. One hundred and fifty years ago, none of this seemed possible: it was to take almost fifty years from the first blurred images produced on bits of treated metal by Nicéphore Niepce and Louis-Jacques Mandé Daguerre, to the possibility of actually recording a simple daily event at the moment of its happening.

Once the major problem of how actually to seize the reflected light, and render it visible and permanent had been solved, the very nature of the technique developed then determined what could be captured, and how it would be reproduced. The daguerreotype, an image on polished metal, that could only be seen if the light was reflected off the plate at a certain angle, became a giddy new toy and the beginnings of an industry of international proportions. Its limitations were enormous, for it required laborious chemical preparation, much of which had to be done in total darkness, a supply of highly polished metal plates, a range of laboratory equipment and a room that could be made absolutely lightproof. This was merely sufficient to produce the surface on which the image would appear; we have not yet even considered the camera. The early daguerreotypes, c. 1840, needed exposures ranging from 15 minutes to an hour and equipment weighing up to 150 lbs. Naturally, total immobility was required of the model, which, in effect, precluded all but the most rigid arrangement of people or objects. Thus, most of the daguerreotypes made during the two decades of their greatest popularity were either very formal studio portraits or landscapes and cityscapes. And even in the latter, any people moving in the streets were rendered as mysterious ectoplasmic blurs. The limitations of highly cumbersome and costly equipment, long and precise chemical manipulations and lengthy exposure times kept photography in the hands of professionals maintaining well-equipped and lucrative studios.

The invention of the Calotype by Fox Talbot, patented by him in 1841, allowed unlimited positive prints to be produced from a paper negative and reduced exposure times to a matter of minutes. This softened somewhat the rigid formalism of studio portraiture with its hidden armature of head clamps and arm props, permitting models to be posed in sunlight in natural surroundings, leaning easily against walls or door jambs, or resting their heads on their hands. Having a picture taken became less of an ordeal for the subject as well, since he was no longer required to hold his eyes open without blinking while staring into the sun for as long as twenty minutes. But this speed was gained at the loss of richness of shadow detail and subtlety of tone, and it was not until the 1850s and the development of the collodion wet-plate, that the great epoch of Victorian photography began.

The principle was simple and yielded excellent results. An impeccably clean glass plate was coated with collodion, formed by dissolving gun-cotton in ether or alcohol mixed with silver and iron iodides. This then had to be rapidly and uniformly coated with the light-sensitive emulsion of silver nitrates, the whole process having to be carried out in a dust-free atmosphere of total darkness. The plate then had to be exposed while the emulsion was still wet and forthwith developed and fixed. Wet, the exposure times were brought down to seconds; dry, the plate was as slow as the daguerreotype had been. The equipment necessary to produce and develop a single glass plate might weigh over 100 lbs. The photographer had to provide for himself every test-tube, pan, basin, drop of water and the means to heat or cool it, chemicals, thermometers, a complete supply of all the glass plates he might need, sufficiently protected to avoid costly breakage, plus the enclosure that would ensure absolute darkness.

Those hardy early photographers needed only the inspiration of a task of such monumental proportions to send them dragging horse-drawn carriages full of photographic equipment into the farthest and darkest corners of the Empire. Within five years from the introduction of the wet-plate, Francis Frith undertook his three-stage, 800-mile odyssey into the Nile Valley, to what is now the border of Sudan. Using three cameras, the smallest of which took 8 × 10 inch glass plates and the largest, 16 × 20, he would set up a complete darkroom in the middle of the desert, after a trek of dozens of miles with the equipment strapped to the backs of mules and camels.

Simultaneously, the Bisson brothers of France were climbing the Alps with

Napoleon III's entourage, requiring 25 porters to carry their equipment. They produced a series of exquisitely composed views of the snowy peaks taken at altitudes of over 2,000 metres. It is almost impossible for the average tourist, puffing and out of breath at the top of the Spanish Steps in Rome, with his Leica strung over his shoulder and his pocket bulging with film sufficient to produce several hundred photographs, to conceive of the difficulties and rigours of such expeditions: where temperatures were so extreme that chemicals either boiled away before they could be used, or were frozen, where snow had to be melted by candle flames that could barely burn for insufficient oxygen before the plates could be washed, where manipulations of extreme delicacy and accuracy had to be performed under conditions of such cold, heat, dust, as to be just barely tolerable. And where perhaps dozens of able-bodied men had to be equipped, lodged and fed simply to get the material from place to place.

The horrors of war photography were even more challenging. Roger Fenton set out to cover the Crimean War in a horse-drawn wagon rather ostentatiously called 'The Photographic Carriage'. Although he was not able to work in the thick of battle, capturing cannon-balls in mid-trajectory, or a cavalry charge with the horses' hooves in mid-air, he could concentrate on the great fixed pieces of war, the battle-fields after the battles, the carnage, the wholesale destruction of bridges and railways. For exposures of 10 to 15 seconds, war corpses make excellent models and need no head clamps! Set pieces, of the troops resting, eating and smoking, or being ministered to by the Florence Nightingales, could always be set up when the light, the heat, the battles and the ravages of epidemic permitted.

The pomposity of much of Victorian life as it appears to us today is no more due to the Victorians' pompous self-image than it is to the very nature of the way that these images were immortalized. Give a man enough time to know that he is going to be recorded for posterity, and he will invariably smooth his hair, straighten his tie and assume a noble posture.

Until about 1860, life in photographs always had to be arranged and organized. The arrival of a photographer's van in a village immediately triggered off a wave of curiosity and interest. It would be the event of the day: every citizen would make it a point to pass by at least once and watch the goings-on; the more leisurely pace of village life would permit a good part of the population to stand around gossiping and staring until the van actually packed up and left. These people would have to be asked to leave, if it was merely an architectural study that was wanted, or they would have to be incorporated into the view and begged to stay while the exposure was being made, or possibly even be coaxed into taking desired poses. Or they could be ignored, in which case, the several-second exposure time would produce interesting amputations of legs from bodies as people ambled across streets, or ghostly blurs, as children played tag around trees.

In the 1860s the first small hand cameras appeared, including one model called the Pistolgraph because it had a spring shutter released by a trigger, and the word 'snap shot', coined by Sir John Herschel, was heard for the first time. The next important evolution came during the 1870s, with the invention of the dry-plate. At last the light-sensitive surface could be produced well in advance of being used, and could be stored until needed. The photographer was freed from the necessity of bringing his own darkroom with him wherever he went. Exposure times of less than a second were also achieved, and the age of documentary photography was about to begin.

By the 1880s, the industrial production of dry-plates and small inexpensive hand cameras had made photography a popular hobby, and with the rise of the Eastman empire, a conception of photography that is still understood in millions of families throughout the world developed. With the invention of the cellulose-based film rolled onto a bobbin and sold in pre-cut lengths to be developed and printed by the maker, and the fixed focus camera with only one speed and one stop, no more was demanded of the interested amateur than one eye and one flexible digit.

The last great achievement of Victorian photography owed its success, however, not to the simplicity of its equipment, but more to the devotion and passion of the man behind it. Paul Martin, from 1892 onwards, using a hand-held plate camera that by today's standards would be considered mammoth, produced a series of unposed documents of the street life of London, with its panoply of trades, markets, accidents, disasters, festivals and jubilees, that was probably the precursor of twentieth-century photojournalism. There, at last, was daily life in all its spontaneity and fragility, the light reflected from an ephemeral particle of time, fixed and rendered timeless.

List of photographers

Abdullah Frères, Constantinople *157*; Barraud, William *7, 9, 14, 47*; Bedford, Francis (1816–94) *112*; Bourne, Samuel (1834–1912) *153*; Bradshaw, W. S. *95*; Cameron, Julia Margaret (1815–79) *19*; Cardesi & Montecchi *121*; Carroll, Lewis (Rev. C. L. Dodgson, 1832–98) *148*; Cundall, Joseph (1818 95) and Downes *28*; Davison, George (1856–1930) *127*; Delamotte, Philip Henry (1820–89) *163*; Emerson, P. H. (1856–1936) *128*; Fenton, Roger (1819–69) *158*; Frith, Francis (1822–98) *50, 58, 68, 76, 109, 110, 113, 115, 123, 150*; Hennah, T. H. *155*; Hill, David Octavius (1802–70) and Adamson, Robert (1821–48) *40, 125*; Hollyer, Frederick H. (1837–1933) *18, 21*; Marion & Co. *20*; Martin, Paul (1864–1942) *77, 94, 111, 164, 175*; Mayall, John Jabez Edwin (1810–1901) *2*; Phené Spiers, R. *86, 146, 147, 149*; Sutcliffe, Frank Meadow, Hon FRPS, (1893–1941) *29, 43, 55, 56, 79, 126*; Talbot, William Henry Fox (1800–77) *51, 133*; Taunt, Henry William *10, 33, 38, 96, 117, 124, 129, 131, 169*; Thomson, John (1837–1921) *22, 39, 44, 75, 84, 89, 90, 92, 100, 103, 134, 177*; Valentine, James (1815–80) *11*; Walker, Samuel A. *165*; Wilson, George Washington (1823–93) *17, 52, 98, 116, 119*.

Photographic acknowledgments

Aberdeen Public Library 17, 52, 98, 116, 119; Aerofilms Library 108, 145, 168, 177; Dr Barnardo's 104; The Curators of The Bodleian Library, Oxford 2, 143, 146, 147, 149; British Museum, Department of Prints and Drawings 181; Conway Picture Library, Greenwich 93, 97, 106; Edinburgh Public Libraries 40, 125, 169; Gernsheim Collection, University of Texas 148; Greater London Council, Photographic Unit, Department of Architecture and Civic Design 54; Greenwich, London Borough of, Local History Library 91; Guildhall Library, City of London 13, 24, 61, 62, 64, 66, 80, 81, 82, 85, 95, 99, 101, 102, 107, 114; Hammersmith Public Library 27; John Hillelson Agency Ltd 3, 4, 6, 37, 50, 60, 75, 84, 89, 90, 92, 100, 103, 120, 122, 134, 137, 142, 154, 159, 161, 177; India Office Library and Records 136; Kodak Museum 15, 36, 127; Museum of English Rural Life, University of Reading 32, 118, 132, 144; National Maritime Museum, Greenwich 45, 70, 178; Oman, Colin 157; Oxford City Libraries 10, 33, 38, 96, 117, 124, 129, 131, 169; Paul Popper Ltd 5, 30, 31, 78, 83, 152, 162, 173; Radio Times Hulton Picture Library 12, 23, 48, 49, 173; Royal Photographic Society 133, 153, 155, 160; Science Museum, London 51, 58, 69, 72, 73; St Bride Printing Library 26; Tower Hamlets Amenities Committee 71, 167, 172; Victoria and Albert Museum 25, 35, 53, 63, 65, 77, 87, 94, 111, 121, 128, 130, 135, 138, 139, 140, 141, 158, 163, 164, 165, 170, 175; Winstone, Reece, AIBP, ARPS, FRSA 16, 34, 42, 59, 74, 88, 105, 176, 179.

1 GEORGE CRUIKSHANK'S ETCHING 'The British Bee Hive' was designed in 1840 and brought up to date by him in 1867. Political and social stratification are identical, with the Royal Family, Parliament, the Law and the Church at the top, the professions in the middle and trade and labour at the bottom. The whole edifice rests on the Bank of England and the Army and Navy.

The British Bee Hive

THIS SECTION FOLLOWS the divisions of Cruikshank's Bee Hive, from Queen to cabman. For most of Victoria's reign English society was remarkably stable. Slum conditions, exploited labour and poverty troubled the conscience of some of the middle classes, but there was very slow radical challenge from below.

2 Victoria and Albert at home. They were married in 1840, when both were only twenty; there were nine children in seventeen years.

3 The widowed Queen Victoria visits Kelso, 21 August 1867. For many years after Prince Albert's death in 1861, the Queen rarely appeared in public.

'The Royal Family by Lineal Descent'

4 The Queen with her grand-daughter Victoria, child of Princess Alice of Hesse, and grandmother of the present Duke of Edinburgh.

5 The Queen's grandson, later George V, and Princess Mary, with their eldest child, the future Duke of Windsor.

'The Aristocracy' *6* Lord Lytton, Viceroy of India, 1875–80. Son of
the novelist Bulwer-Lytton, he had a distinguished
diplomatic career and received an earldom in 1880.

7 Lady Randolph Churchill, by Barraud. She was
American by birth, married Lord Randolph in
January 1874 and became the mother of Winston
Churchill in November.

'Freedom to all Religious Denominations'

8 The Church of England: the Bishop of Bath and Wells (Rt. Hon. Rt. Rev. Lord Arthur Charles Hervey).

9 The Roman Catholic Church: Cardinal Newman, 1888, by Barraud. In 1850 Pius IX had restored the Roman Catholic hierarchy in England.

10 Evangelicalism: Bible stand at St. Giles's Fair, Oxford, 1880, by Henry William Taunt.

'The British Constitution'

11 Mr. Gladstone at a picnic, 16 September 1893. At the age of eighty-four Gladstone was Prime Minister for the fourth time.

12 James Keir Hardie, the first socialist Member of Parliament, wearing his famous cloth cap. Elected in 1892, he was one of the founders of the Independent Labour Party the next year.

'Law and Equity'   *13* Gaolers at Newgate.

14 Rt. Hon. Sir Henry Cotton, Lord Justice of Appeal.

'Schools'   15 Schoolmaster, c. 1898.

16 Classroom in St. George British School, Bristol, 1895. The nineteenth century saw the triumph of publicly financed education. By 1891 free schooling was available to everyone.

'Medical Science'   *17* Operation in progress, using Listerian
antiseptic methods, Aberdeen, 1869. Lister's
emphasis on cleanliness in hospitals saved many
from death by gangrene.

'Chemistry'   *18* Lord Rayleigh (1842–1919). His major work was
concerned with electro-magnetism, optics and
sound.

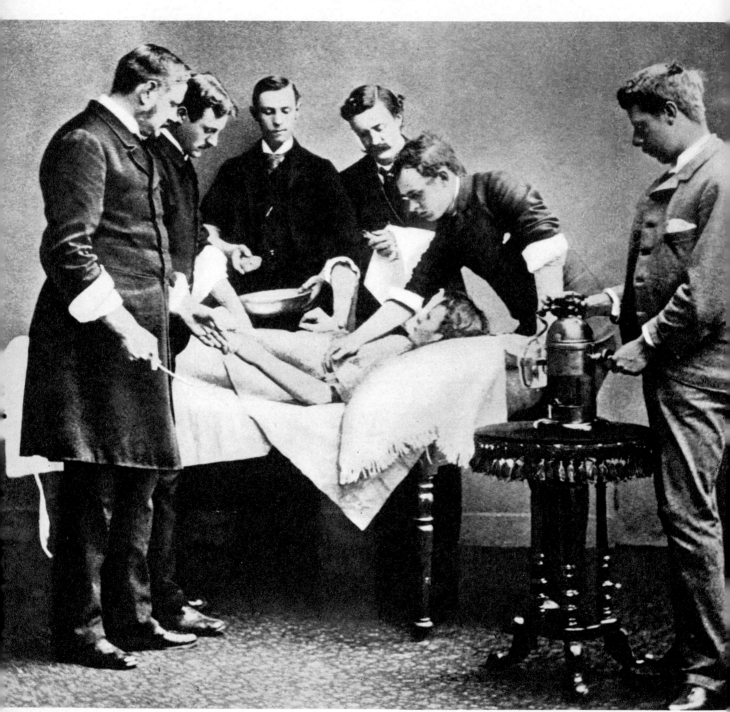

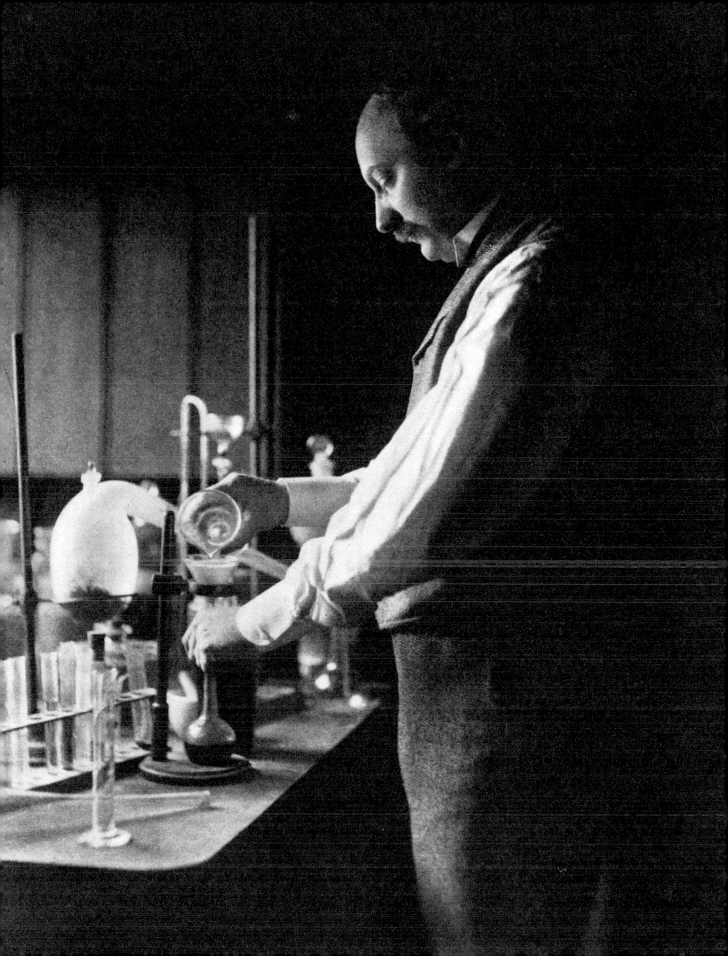

'Art', Commercial and Fine   *22* Sign-painter, 1870, by John Thompson.

23 G. F. Watts in his studio, Kensington. A prolific and successful artist, Watts (1817–1904) was equally esteemed as a portraitist and as a painter of would-be profound allegorical subjects.

'A Free Press, Honest and Independent'

24 Caxton Letter Works, Field Lane, London, 1868.

25 Wood-engravers, 1890s, by Paul Martin. Almost all illustrations in books, magazines and newspapers were reproduced from wood blocks, painstakingly engraved by hand, often at great speed, from artists' drawings or, occasionally, photographs. By the time this picture was taken mechanical processes were rapidly ousting hand methods.

26 David Payne's 'Wharfedale' Printing Press, c. 1850, one of the first rotary presses.

27 Printers at the Kelmscott Press, founded by William Morris to revive the craft of fine printing.

28 A group of foremen at the International Exhibition of 1862, by Cundall and Barnes. The vast exhibition buildings of 1851 and 1862 were as impressive as any of the objects inside.

29 Jet workshop, Whitby, 1890, by F. M. Sutcliffe. Whitby, in Yorkshire, was the principal source of English jet; it was mined in large quantities and carved and polished on lathes.

'Girls and Women'   *30* Housekeeper and domestic servants, 1886.

31 Workers at an iron works in South Wales, 1865. The rights and status of women were subjects of a running debate throughout the nineteenth century.

'Agriculture'

32 Hop-drying at Seddlescombe, Sussex, 1900. The long sacks, or 'pokes', each hold ten bushels of hops. In the oast-houses behind, the hops are laid out on floors and dried by means of stoves at the bottom.

33 A hill-shepherd, survivor from a pre-industrial world untouched by 'progress', by Henry Taunt.

'Invention' *34* Isambard Kingdom Brunel, during the
construction of the Great Eastern, 1857. After a
brilliant career as engineer to the Great Western
Railway, Brunel (1806–59) turned his energies to
large-scale, steam-driven ships.

'Mechanics'   *35* Winch-operator at the building of the
International Exhibition of 1862. These exhibitions
were designed, in the words of the 1862 catalogue,
'to help forward the upward progress of industrial
civilization'.

'Butcher', 'Baker'

36 Farmer Bates, Butcher. The rise of the wholesaler, collecting from the source and redistributing to the retailer, revolutionized nineteenth-century merchandising as much as the supermarket in our time.

37 Ede and Sons, Grocer and Baker. Brand foods had already begun to replace the unpackaged product.

'Boatman', 'Cabman' *38* Abel Beesley, Waterman, near Oxford, c. 1900, by Henry Taunt.

39 'Cast-iron Billy', an ex-omnibus driver, c. 1870, by John Thompson. Billy (William Parragreen), after forty-three years on the road, was dismissed for failing to 'race' the younger men.

'Masons', 'Bricklayers' *40* Masons at work on the Scott Memorial, Edinburgh, from the Hill-Adamson album. The memorial to Walter Scott, erected in 1844, was one of the earliest and grandest of Neo-Gothic monuments.

41 Tile-hangers and bricklayers, 1890s.

'Paviors'   *42* Roadmen at Redlands, Bristol, 1854.

'Sweep'   *43* Chimney-sweeps, Whitby, by T. M. Sutcliffe.
Sweeps once made an additional income by
selling the soot as fertilizer and pesticide.

'The Army, the Navy and the Volunteers'

44 Recruiting sergeants, Westminster, 1870, by John Thompson. The Army had to rely on the persuasion of such men as these. New recruits, having accepted the Queen's shilling, were allowed four days to think over their bargain.

45 Captain H. Rushton, R.N. He was Captain Coxswain of H.M.S. *Edinburgh* at the Diamond Jubilee Review, Spithead, 1897.

'Bank of the Richest Country in the World'

46 Old Dividend Office, Bank of England, 1894. The Bank had been founded as far back as 1694. In the later nineteenth century its chief function was to maintain a proper balance between the supply of credit and stocks of gold. Sir John Soane's very fine banking halls of 1788–1808, of which this is one, were demolished in the twenties of this century.

Queen Bees

47 Adelina Patti in 1880. An American of Spanish parentage, Patti excelled in Italian operatic roles. She married three times, the last to a Swedish baron.

48 Marie Lloyd, darling of the English music-hall.

49 Charity matinée at the Theatre Royal,
Haymarket, 1899. Fashionable audiences flocked
to light, drawing-room comedies, though Bernard
Shaw was already crusading for Ibsen and the
'new drama'.

Iron and Steam

BRITAIN WAS THE FIRST COUNTRY in the world to feel the full impact of industrialization. It brought wealth, technical triumphs, agonizing social problems . . . and above all, change. A new world was being created, hailed as a golden age by some, detested as the ultimate barbarism by others. The photographers, like the public at large, were fascinated, and their pictures catch a sense of that half-fearful wonder which can perhaps never be recaptured.

50 The Forth Railway Bridge, c. 1890. After the Tay Bridge disaster of 1879, improved engineering techniques were developed and used here for the first time.

51 Nelson's Column, 1844, by Fox Talbot. The column had been erected in 1842; here the relief panels are being added to the base. Landseer's lions did not follow until the 1860s.

Achievement in Stone

52 Steam stone-cutting machine at Tilly Fourie Quarry, Aberdeen, 1880.

53 The new Palace of Westminster, designed by Charles Barry and A. W. N. Pugin. Begun in 1839, it was not finished until 1860. Gothic in style (to suggest links with England's medieval past), it incorporated the most up-to-date techniques of fire-proofing, ventilation, etc.

The Architecture of the Future

54 The Crystal Palace being re-erected at Sydenham, 1853. Paxton's Crystal Palace, a revolutionary design in iron and glass which foreshadowed modern architecture, had been erected in Hyde Park for the Great Exhibition of 1851. It was rebuilt, with major changes, at Sydenham, and burned down in 1936.

Forging the Rail Network

55 Building the Whitby to Loftus line, early 1880s. Cutting, tunnel and track are finished, and the line is almost ready to be opened.

56 Building a viaduct between Whitby and Scarborough, early 1880s. Notice the man in the diving-suit on the right.

The Palace of *King Coal*   *57* Lime Street Station, Liverpool, 1880. Built in 1867 to the designs of Baker and Stevenson, its span of 200 feet was at that time the widest in the world. But it was surpassed almost at once by St. Pancras.

Bridge Builders

58 The Royal Albert Bridge, Saltash, Devon, 1858. This was part of Brunel's Great Western line to Penzance. It consists of two huge trusses, built on the ground and raised into position, the first in 1857, the second (shown here) the following year.

59 Clifton Suspension Bridge, Bristol, under construction, 1863. Also by Brunel, though completed after his death. The chains, from which the road is to be suspended, came from the demolished Hungerford Bridge, London.

60 A viaduct on the Barnstaple to Lynton line, North Devon. Note the wooden centering still in position under the right-hand arch.

Overleaf: **Landscapes of Iron**

61 King's Cross Station, London, built in 1851–52 as the terminal of the Great Northern Railway.

62 Boiler house of the City of London Electric Lighting Co., Bankside.

Studies in Scaffolding

63 The International Exhibition Building of 1862 under construction in October 1861. For an interior view see pl. 171.

64 Building the Metropolitan Railway, Baker Street, July 1862. This was the first underground railway in the world, and ran from Paddington to Farringdon Street. It opened in 1863.

On Site *65* Engineers supervising the boilers for the International Exhibition of 1862.

66 Ladies visiting Holborn Viaduct, 1870. A small point of interest is that the lady holds her umbrella by what seems to us the wrong end, the gentleman by the handle.

Flyover

67 Holborn Viaduct nearing
completion, 1870. Before this
the road dipped steeply down
to the Fleet Valley and up
again. The new bridge was
designed by William Heywood,
the City Engineer.

Wheels of Power

68 The Laxey Wheel, near Douglas, Isle of Man, 1897. The 'Big Wheel' was built in 1854 to operate the pumps of a lead mine. It works by hydraulic power, water from a nearby hill reservoir being channelled into the tower.

69 Boydell's Traction Engine. Steam traction engines served a variety of purposes. This one has been adapted for muddy ground by primitive caterpillar tracks.

The *Great Eastern* 70 Richard Tangye with one of his hydraulic presses used in the launching, 1858.

71 On board, 1858. The *Great Eastern* was Brunel's last and greatest ship; 692 feet long, weighing 22,500 tons, she was driven by both propellers and paddle-wheels.

The Conquest of Land, Sea and Air

72 Sir Hiram Maxim's Flying Machine, 1894. It was powered by steam, reached a speed of 36 m.p.h. and flew for about 300 feet.

73 Garrett's Submarine, 1880, the invention of the Rev. G. W. Garrett. Submarines had already been used effectively in the American Civil War.

74 Early motor-cars at Bristol, 1898.

Town and Country

In THE TOWNS the pace of life quickened; competition grew keener, enterprise burgeoned. In the country technology was slower in making its impact, but traditional ties were being loosened; and as a specifically rural way of life faded, it became the object of a nostalgic quest which has still not quite come to an end.

75 Covent Garden Market, 1870. Flowers and vegetables arrived in fashionable Covent Garden as early as the seventeenth century.

76 Hop-pickers in Kent, 1900. The hop harvest provided an annual paid holiday for the Cockneys of London's East End.

London Streets

77 Magazine-seller at Ludgate
Circus, 1890s. With the spread
of literacy, cheap popular
magazines were beginning to
build up a mass readership.

78 The Strand, about 1900.
Traffic was already a problem,
and new roads like Charing
Cross Road and Queen
Victoria Street were changing
the face of London.

The Art of Advertising

79 'Boardie Willie' by F. M. Sutcliffe. The boardman's life, wrote one observer, was 'a means of subsistence open to the most stupid and forlorn of individuals'.

80, 81, 82 Bill-boards at King's Cross Station, 1862; Ludgate Hill, 1900; and Holborn Viaduct, 1869. In the last example notice not only the Midland Railway's announcement of 'new St. Pancras Station', but also the elastic lettering of the rubber advertisement next to it.

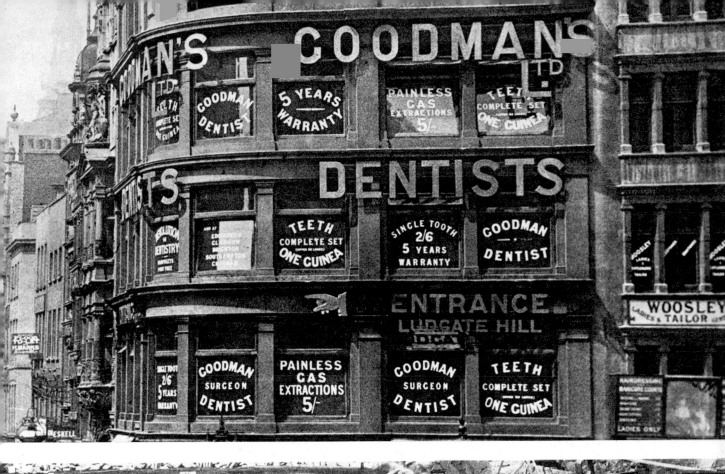

The Horse in Town

83 Omnibus outside the National Gallery, London. The double-decker bus evolved from the stage-coach, with its accommodation on the roof; the staircase was a late development.

84 Selling strawberries, 1877. The fruit came not from the country but from Covent Garden Market. 'On a 'ot night', said one costermonger, 'I'd rather sell 'em than eat 'em.'

85 A Hansom cab – the 'gondola of London' – outside the Old Bell Inn, 1884. The driver sat in a high seat behind.

The New Hospitality *86* Belle Vue Hotel, an example of the modern, well-organized hotel where it was a treat to stay.

87 The Tabard Inn, Southwark. The old-style inn made no pretence of being more than an overnight stopping place.

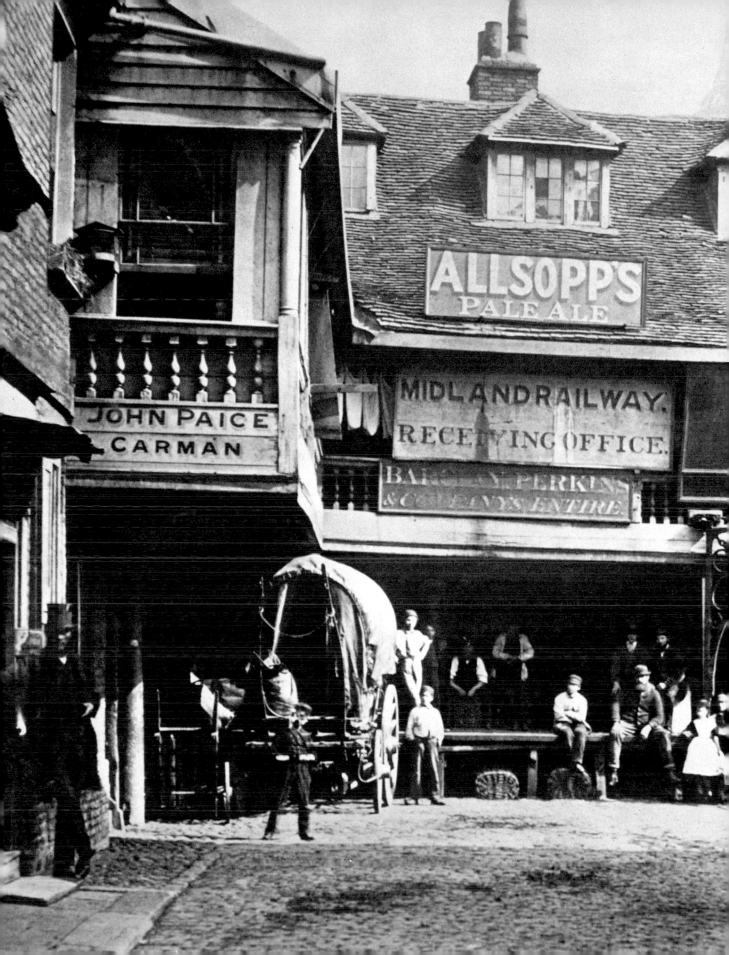

'Who'll Buy?' *88* Brush and shoe shops in Mary le Port Street, Bristol, late 1890s. The best advertisement was still to display as many of your wares as you could get on to the pavement.

89 Second-hand furniture, 1870s. Such a shop would cater for the very poor, acquiring its wares from bailiffs and pawnbrokers.

The Life of the Streets

90 Flower-sellers outside St. Paul's, Covent Garden, 1870s, by John Thompson. A flower-girl questioned by Henry Mayhew about 1850 'used to be out frequently till past midnight, and seldom or never got home before nine'.

91 Crossing-sweeper, Greenwich. In the days of muddy roads, crossing-sweepers could live on the tips of local residents.

92 Dealer in imitation jewellery, 1877. The man told Thompson, who took the photograph: 'I have sold two dozen wedding-rings in a night, some for a lark, others for weddings, and a lot to wear in place of the genuine wedding-rings pawned for a drink, so as not to let the husband know.'

93 Selling rabbits, Greenwich, 1885.

94 Knife-grinder, 1890. The grindstone was expensive. Many 'tinmen' spent half their takings on hiring one.

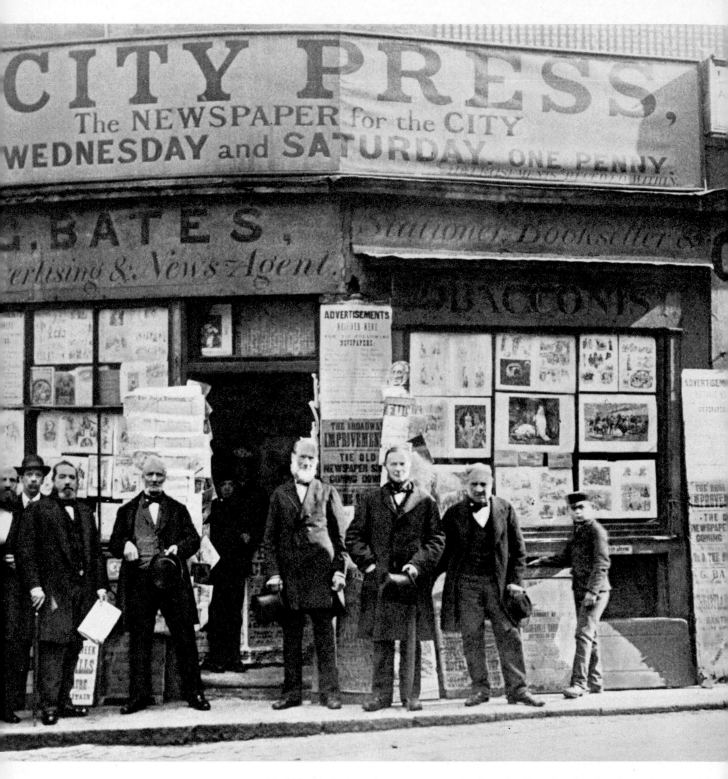

Public Prints   *95* Newsagent's shop in Farringdon Street, also selling prints and probably stationery.

96 Henry Taunt's own shop in Oxford, with road-menders at work outside.

Public Services

97 Greenwich Fire Brigade, 1885. When answering a call the man at the back stoked the boiler to work the pump, while the one to the left of the driver called out to clear the way. He was known as the 'Hi! hi! man'.

98 Ward in the Royal Infirmary, Aberdeen, 1890s. Florence Nightingale was still alive, in her seventies, ruling the nursing profession from her couch with an iron hand.

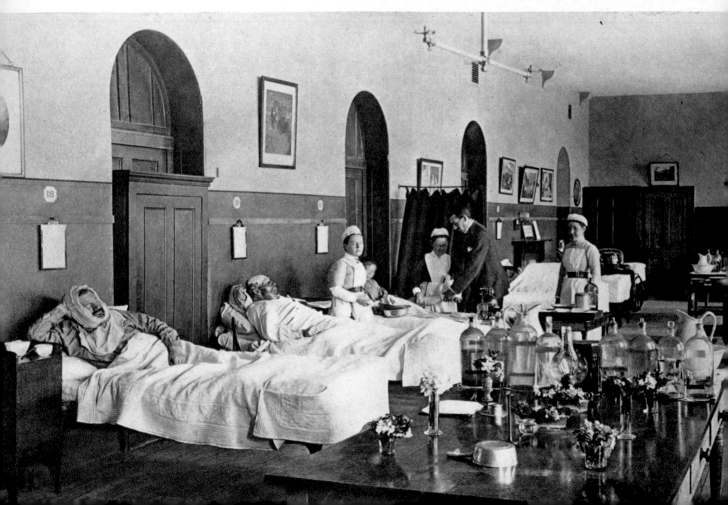

99 A Londoner helping the police with their enquiries. The Metropolitan Police Force had been received with considerable uneasiness at first, but by the end of the century had won the public's trust and co-operation.

100 Public disinfectors, 1877, by John Thompson. When a case of smallpox was identified, it was their job to collect all the clothes, bedding, carpets and curtains of the house and take them to an oven where they were heated to 280 degrees.

London's Underprivileged

101 Vegetable stall in Shoe Lane, 1871. Street stalls were far more specialized than today. One would sell only watercress, another nothing but peas. At Houndsditch a whole market was devoted to oranges, lemons and nuts.

102 White Hind Alley, Bankside, 1896. Artisan dwellings, poor but respectable.

Overleaf:

103 'The crawler', 1877, one of Thompson's most moving photographs. The old woman was completely destitute, slept on the stone steps of the workhouse and spent the day looking after a friend's baby in return for a cup of tea and some bread.

104 Homeless boys on admission to Dr. Barnardo's Home, about 1880.

Bristol in the Nineties

105 Crew's Hole, St. George, Bristol, 1890s. Various industries had established themselves on the banks of the Avon. The woman is drawing water.

Railway Comfort

106 Railway guard, South Eastern Railway, 1885. The guard's uniform and the fine workmanship of the carriage indicate the industry's justifiable pride. Third-class carriages, though, still had wooden seats and were unheated and unlit.

107 Epsom Downs Station, 1898. Can the stout gentleman on the right, the object of widespread interest, be the Prince of Wales?

Away From It All

108 Paddling. The benefits of sea bathing had been discovered, or invented, in the late eighteenth century, but it was not until the railway age that the people as a whole could enjoy it.

109 The pier at Deal, 1899, a study in composition and in mood.

110 Ventnor Railway Station, Isle of Wight. The popularity of the Isle of Wight was no doubt increased by Victoria and Albert's residence at Osborne. Tennyson too lived near Freshwater. But it developed relatively slowly. A guide-book published as late as 1905 was forced to admit that

'the accommodation afforded by the railway
station leaves much to be desired. It is only fair
to the officials, however, to say that passengers
receive every attention that can be expected.'
Ventnor was the terminus of the Isle of Wight
Railway, which began at Ryde.

Holiday Pleasures   *111* Punch and Judy show on the beach at Ilfracombe, 1894, by Paul Martin.

112 Sidmouth Promenade, 1870s, by Francis Bedford. Bathers had to change in the bathing huts, which were then wheeled into the sea and one descended into the water from steps.

Overleaf: *113* The Pavilion, Buxton, 1871. Buxton's development as a spa culminated in the building of the Pavilion, 'a provincial Crystal Palace, comprising a concert hall, a conservatory and a large lounge, and serving as a promenade when the weather is unfavourable'.

The Market *114* Floral Hall, Covent Garden Market. The market system was (and is) a survival from pre-industrial England, and London's markets were only larger and more specialized examples. In 1877 two thousand porters were employed in flowers alone.

115 Cattle market at Llanrwst, near Conway, Wales.

Old Inhabitants

116 On Skye, 1830. In the country old age was perhaps slightly less to be dreaded because communities were more tightly knit. There was no old-age pension until 1908.

117 At Dorchester, Oxford-shire.

118 At Stratton, Cornwall. The man on the far right is said to have been a drummer-boy at Waterloo.

Hunting, Shooting and Fishing

Field sports were another eighteenth-century gentleman's pursuit avidly taken over by the Victorian upper classes, whatever their social background.

119 A stag from the royal forests of Glen Etive, 1880. The opening-up of the Highlands was due to the railways, the novels of Walter Scott and the example of the Royal Family, in roughly equal proportions.

120 Shooting party, 1890.

121 Mr. Raply and 'Cruiser', 1858.

122 Colonel Grey fishing at the Bridge of Dee.

Backwaters *123* Boating parties on the Thames, at Molesey
Lock, near Hampton, 1896.

124 James Lowe, lock-keeper, by Henry Taunt.

Boatmen

125 Fisherman at Newhaven, Edinburgh, 1845, from the Hill-Adamson collection.

126 Fishermen on the beach at Whitby, an evocation of sea and sky as powerful as any realist painting.

127 Canal barge, 1900. It is being loaded with bundles of wood. The barge-horse stands nearby.

128 Eel-fishing, 1886. The man sets the bow net, the wife rows.

The Daily Round

129 Milkman, Llandudno, by Henry Taunt, 1895. Milk came straight from cow to consumer in churns.

130 Chatting with the postman. The picture would seem posed, were it not for the lady on the right who is clearly waiting for a letter.

131 The Burford bus outside the Bull, c. 1890, by Henry Taunt.

132 Tradesmen delivering goods, Willersey, Worcestershire, c. 1900. A scene like this already looked quaint and old-fashioned, and was no doubt photographed for that very reason.

Established, Unestablished

133 Old gamekeeper at Lacock Abbey, c. 1845, by William Fox Talbot

134 Gypsies at Battersea, 1877, by John Thompson. A macabre detail: the woman sitting on the steps was murdered four weeks after the photograph was taken.

Home and Abroad

ONE OF THE FASCINATIONS of the Victorian age is the way it took the British
way of life to the ends of the earth, and established it so firmly that in many
cases it has remained after the tide of empire receded. Victorian manners,
strictly instilled at home, seem to have been serenely unaffected by climate,
custom and crisis.

135 Young girl reading at Adair
Manor, Ireland, 1860.

136 Tea on the lawn. Only the turbans
betray the fact that we are in India.

The Queen's Birthday

137 Queen Victoria's
Birthday Table, Balmoral,
24 May 1873. She was fifty-five.
The presents are largely
portraits of her children and
grandchildren.

Below Stairs, Above Stairs *138* Servants of an upper middle-class household. They are probably four married couples, the oldest the butler and housekeeper, the youngest (on the right) the handyman and housemaid.

139 Drawing-room of Broom House, Fulham, 1860s
– an eighteenth-century home furnished in the
heavier taste of a later age. Many of the chairs
have slip-covers for protection.

140 Tea-party, 1865: the formality of the drawing-room (notice the upholstered sofa for the older ladies) transferred to the romantic setting of a landscape garden.

Beau Monde and Demi-Monde

141 Another tea-party, c. 1860. The social class is not as clear as in the previous photograph, but there is a distinctly gayer air.

142 Sarah Brown, a popular music-hall dancer. She was gaoled for three months on a charge of indecency for wearing this costume.

The World of the Child   *143* A sedate ride in the donkey cart.

144 Toy-making at home, c. 1900. The whole family are making curious bird-dolls. Even the baby seems to be trying his hand with the thread.

145 Groups of children, 1895. The boys in the foreground are evidently poor, and the better-off children behind know it.

Children at Home

146 The dining-room of No. 14 St. Giles's Street, Oxford, 1857, by R. Phené Spiers.

147 'Interior of a tent, 90 degrees in the shade', 1857, by R. Phené Spiers. These two pictures, and the one opposite, are of the photographer's own family.

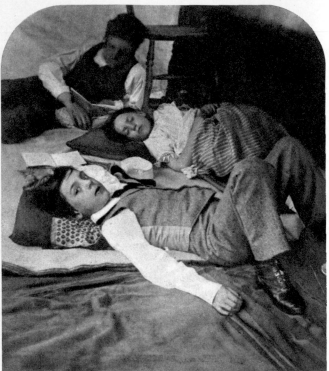

148 'It won't come smooth' – a portrait of Irene MacDonald, by Lewis Carroll, 1863.

149 Charlotte Spiers gazing into a mirror, 1857.
Spiers excelled in these meditative pictures,
making a virtue of long exposures and static poses.

En Voyage   *150* The S.S. *Duchess of York* at Folkestone, 1896.
On the right the train has come to meet the
Channel steamer.

151 Swabbing the decks of the S.S. *Illawarra*, 1881.

152 Potato and spoon race, passengers on a cruise
to Norway, 1896.

England Overseas   *153* Oakaver, Simla, 1867, by Samuel Bourne. The garden consists entirely of potted plants.

154 Tea on the terrace of Archie Chamberlin's bungalow, India, 1878.

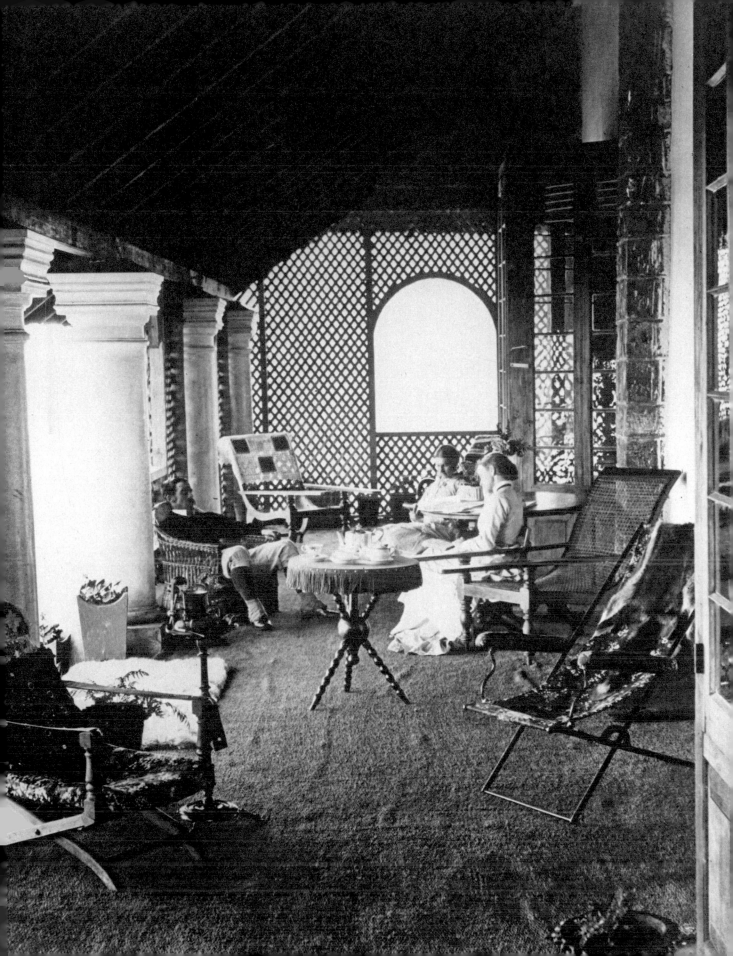

Cricket Goes to the New World *155* The English cricket team leaves for America, 1859.

Going Native *156* Ordnance Survey Team in Sinai, 1868–69. All are English except the two Egyptian servants wearing the fez.

157 English ladies at Constantinople, 1876.

The Face of War *158* Camp of the Dragoon Guards outside Sebastopol, with French and English soldiers. Roger Frenton was the first photo-journalist, and his pictures of the Crimea had a strong impact at home.

159 Preparing for a route march in South Africa, near Port Elizabeth, c. 1880. The Boer War is still twenty years away.

160 Ladysmith, 30 October 1899, at the very beginning of the four-month siege. Photography can now record history as it happens.

The Call of the Mountains

161 Prince Arthur's expedition to Mt. Blanc, 1865. Alpinism was a great focus of public excitement. In this same year the Matterhorn was climbed for the first time.

162 Climbing in the French Alps, 1880. Notice the unflappable pipe-smoker on the ladder.

A Day to Remember

THIS FINAL SECTION is devoted to special occasions, from royal jubilees to family outings. It is a record, on the whole, of peace and pleasure, for the Victorian photographer, like many artists of all ages (until the present), tended to represent life as slightly more interesting, colourful and agreeable than it probably really was.

163 The opening of the Crystal Palace after its re-erection at Sydenham, 1855. On the platform are the Emperor Napoleon III, Queen Victoria, the Empress Eugénie and Prince Albert.
164 Holiday crowd on Yarmouth Sands, 1892.

Fire and Frost *165* Her Majesty's Theatre, after the fire which destroyed it on 6 December 1867.

166 The Thames below Limehouse during the Great Frost of February 1895.

Sporting Scenes

167 W. G. Grace going in to bat. Grace was famous in first-class cricket for thirty-six years (1865–1900), on one occasion scoring 224 not out.

168 Cyclists of the Queen's City of Edinburgh Rifle Volunteer Brigade in George Street, Edinburgh, 1884. The large wheel of the penny-farthing had the same effect as a gear, before the introduction of the bicycle chain.

169 Spectators at Henley Regatta, 1898, by Henry Taunt.

On Show to the World

170 Exhibition at Exeter School of Art, 1857.

171 Part of the International Exhibition of 1862. The fountain in the foreground is made of Minton majolica tiles, the screen behind it is Gilbert Scott's for Hereford Cathedral, and the organ at the back is by Henry Willis.

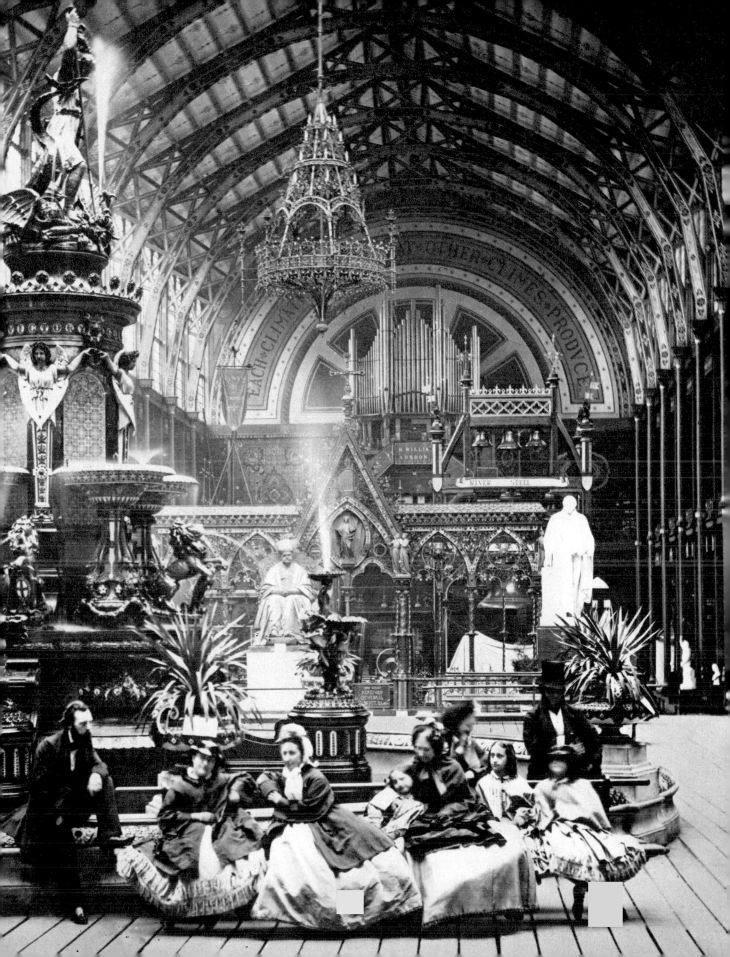

'God Bless this Ship'

172 The launching of H.M.S. *Albion* from the Thames Iron Works, 1898.

173 Queen Victoria, a tiny figure in black, launching H.M.S. *Royal Sovereign*, 26 February 1891. On the Queen's right is the Prince of Wales.

Fun at the Fair   *174* Slot-machines on a pier.

175 Hampstead Fair, 1898.

Show and Side-Show   *176* Barnum and Bailey's Circus comes to Bristol, 15 August 1898. It was P. T. Barnum who invented the phrase 'The Greatest Show on Earth'. It included acrobats, animal acts, 'freaks' and clowns, and toured the world from 1871 to 1907.

177 November effigies, London, 1877, by John Thompson. Guy Fawkes was not the only unpopular figure to be burned in effigy – the Pope, Cardinal Wiseman and the Tsar of Russia were also so honoured. This one is called by Thompson 'a meaningless monstrosity'.

Sixty Glorious Years   *178* Sailors at Spithead, Diamond Jubilee, 1897.

179 Broad Street, Bristol, decorated for the Diamond Jubilee. Victoria is the only British monarch to celebrate a reign of more than sixty years. She long outlived any hostility and in her old age was revered as the symbol of Britain's greatness.

The Queen at St. Paul's

180 Diamond Jubilee, 1897;
the procession outside St.
Paul's Cathedral. The Queen's
religion set the pattern for
that of her subjects – deeply
sincere but liberal in outlook
and conscious of 'the rights
of reason and science'.

Gracious Majesty   *181* Unveiling a statue to Queen Victoria, College Green, Bristol, 25 July 1888. In front of the plinth stands the Mayor of Bristol. Facing him, doffing his top hat, is the Prince of Wales's eldest son, the Duke of Clarence, who died in 1892.